SKY GODS

In two masks from British Columbia, the sun (*left*) has a powerful, stern face with curling sun rays and the moon (*above*) has a gentle female face. (See "North American Indians," pp. 38-44.)

Right: Thoth, a dog-headed baboon, was the Egyptian god of wisdom and science who watched over the night sky. In this 8th-century B.C. ceramic statue, he is crowned with both a full and a crescent moon. (See "Egypt," pp. 28-37.)

Overleaf: An 18th-century Indian painting of a sun disk representing the sun god Surya, who crossed the sky in his golden chariot. (See "India," pp. 16-21.)

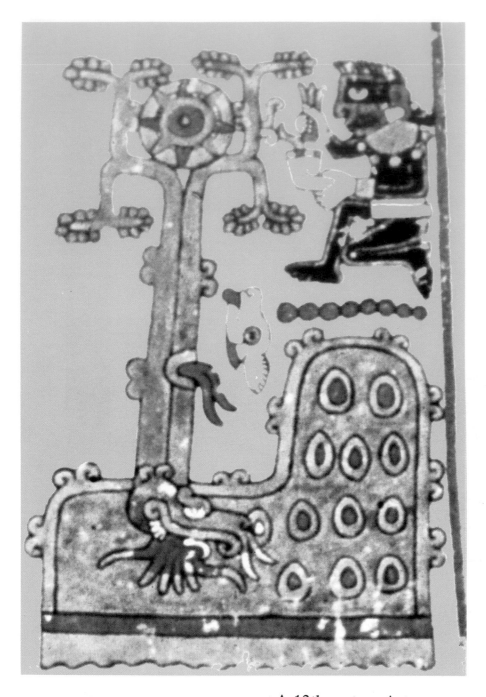

Right: An 18th-century emperor's robe showing (*above*) the hare on the moon mixing the drink of immortality, and (*below*) the great dragon. (See "China," pp. 74-83.)

A 13th-century Aztec painting showing the sun god feeding on the hearts of sacrificed enemy warriors, while the sun glows as a great flower in the upper tree branches. (See "Aztecs," pp. 52-57.)

Above: The Japanese
believe that devils and ghosts
exist in neon-lighted Tokyo
as well as in the wooded
countryside. This late-
18th-century painting on
silk shows the devil chased
by the red sun. (See
"Japan," pp. 58-63.)

Right: In this 18th-century
painting, Surya, the three-
eyed Hindu sun god,
enclosed in the symbol of the
sun, carries a sword to kill
evil demons. (See "India,"
pp. 16-21.)

A Nazca mask of beaten gold representing the sun. (See "Incas," pp. 70-73.)

SKY GODS

the sun and moon in art and myth

by Katherine Komaroff

UNIVERSE BOOKS
New York

design by Ira Friedlander

Published in the United States of America in 1974
by Universe Books, 381 Park Avenue South, New York, N.Y. 10016
© 1974 by Universe Books
Library of Congress Catalog Card Number: 73-80052
ISBN 0-87663-187-1
Printed in the United States of America

To my family

Contents

Introduction

Imagine! It is a morning just like any other morning. You wake up as usual. But today you sense that something is very different. . . . *The sun is not up with you!* You think that you must still be half asleep and dreaming . . . but you are completely awake, and it is indeed morning although it is as dark as midnight. There isn't even a moon. All over the world, animals scurry about nervously, aware that something is very wrong.

Suddenly you realize how important the sun is and how much we take it for granted. But what do we really know about it? What exactly is the sun? What is the moon? Where do they come from? Where do they go? Why does the moon change its shape? Are they even real?

Ever since the beginning of time, man has wondered about the meaning and behavior of the sun and moon. He has carefully observed their cycles and realized their importance for his own survival. The close contact with nature that ancient man enjoyed made him more conscious of their presence, whether he lived in a place constantly warmed by the sun or in a bitter cold world where the sun seemed far away.

Ancient men tried to explain the meaning of this mysterious phenomenon in stories closely related to their own lives and their religious beliefs. The Hindu people of India said that the sun was a red man with four arms in a golden chariot; the Egyptians said that the sun was a great watchful eye; the North American Indians said that the moon was a great ball of light tossed into the sky by a clever creature called Raven; and the Eskimos believed that the moon was a powerful hunter who often stood in front of his igloo.

These stories, called myths, are handed down from generation to generation, and celebrate the great mystery of life. They are loved because of their beauty and power and also for what they tell us about people of other cultures.

In this book you will find myths and art that people of many different civilizations created to express their beliefs about the sun and the moon.

INDIA
surya and sanjna

Every day, on an invisible path high in the heavens, a golden chariot crosses the sky. In this glittering chariot is a dark red man with three eyes and four arms. His chariot is drawn by seven magnificent horses, and a legless charioteer guides them along their course. The dark red man is very powerful, for he is the Hindu sun god Surya whose light is so bright that we cannot really see him in his chariot. We see only the brilliant glaring ball that surrounds him as he crosses.

Surya married the beautiful and wise goddess Sanjna. In the early years of their marriage, they were happy together and they had two wonderful children, the first man and woman on earth. But time passed and Sanjna became more and more discontent. She began to realize that she was being blinded by her husband's brilliance and overbearing character. She knew that she would have to leave him in order to find her true self.

When Sanjna fled, she left her lovely maid in her place

Surya stands above the seven powerful horses and the legless charioteer in this 12th-century Indian stone sculpture. Beside him are less powerful gods who help him drive away darkness at the beginning of each day.

17

The wheels of the sun chariot temple at Konarak in India, each ten feet in diameter, symbolize the eternal cycle of the sun.

so that Surya would not miss her. Sanjna disguised herself as a mare and went to live in a quiet forest where she could devote herself to meditation. For some time, Surya didn't even know that she had gone. But when he did notice, he longed to be with her again. He had not meant to make her unhappy and he began to search for her everywhere.

One day he saw a mare grazing peacefully in the green fields and he realized that it was Sanjna in her new home. How beautiful she looked! He loved her so much and wanted to share her new found tranquility. So he too left the heavens and took the form of a horse. Sanjna was pleased to see him again and they lived together happily. Their days were long and quiet and the understanding between them deepened.

Built in the shape of a sun chariot, A.D. 1240-80, the great sun temple was erected by King Narasimhadeva I on the site of a miracle performed by the sun god Surya. The entire temple is covered with elaborate carving.

But time passed and they knew that they must return to their places in the heavens. So they changed themselves back into their human forms and saying goodbye to the soft green forest that had mended their divine love, they went back to the sky.

The whole world rejoiced when they returned together. No one wanted them to separate again, least of all Sanjna's father, who cared deeply about her happiness. So the wise father shaved away enough of Surya's brilliance so that Sanjna would never again feel the need to flee from him. The fragments of brilliance that had been shaved away were given to the other gods. From these fragments, they received their power. And, in the end, Surya gained greater strength and stability by giving away some of his power.

Above: In this 18th-century painting, Surya's chariot, drawn by seven horses, is guided along its course by a charioteer who represents dawn. Like the first appearance of light in the morning when the day is not yet formed, the charioteer is not fully formed and is legless.

Right: Seven galloping horses pulled Surya's chariot across the sky. Each represented a day of the week. This red sandstone sculpture was carved almost two thousand years ago.

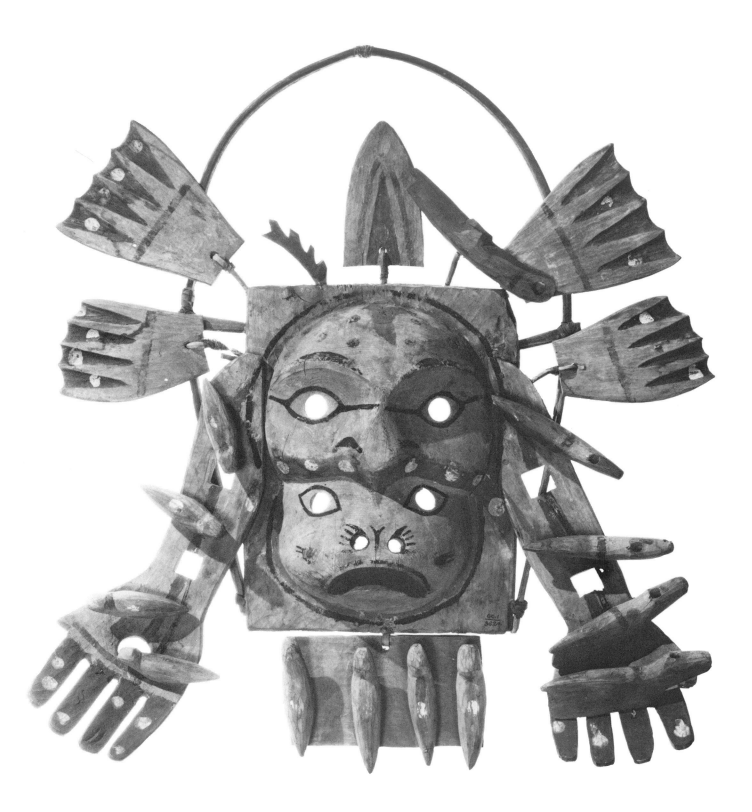

Used in Eskimo ceremonies, this wooden mask from Alaska symbolizes the moon as both a hunter and protector of the seals, which he holds in his hands. He is depicted as a double spirit: the upper eyes and nose represent his human spirit, and the lower eyes, nose, and mouth represent his seal spirit.

ESKIMOS
skywatchers

At the edge of the sky, three stars, like steps cut in a snowbank, link heaven and earth and form, for the Eskimos, the bridge to another world. In this other world, the moon is a powerful hunter and a great fisherman. He has a sled with a team of spotted dogs. Together with his dogs, he hunts for animals and piles his

In Eskimo life, the shaman was a leader who had the magical power of communicating with spirits in nature or in the bodies of animals. When the shaman wore a mask such as these from the Bering Sea area, he could communicate with the spirit represented and thus heal the sick and change the course of natural events. Carved in many forms, the painted wooden masks were made to represent human, fish, or animal spirits.

sled high with their skins. He is often seen standing in front of his igloo. Sometimes one of his dogs sneaks away and leaves the sky to visit earth in the form of a shooting star.

The moon lives in his igloo with his cousin the clown. She often comes out in the night sky and dances to make people laugh. The twinkling star is really the clown winking at the people on earth. But she is a cruel clown, for if any visitor laughs too hard, she may dry him up!

Often the moon chases his beautiful sister, the sun. He tries to catch up with her as she carries her golden torch across the sky. But she is always too far ahead of him, and

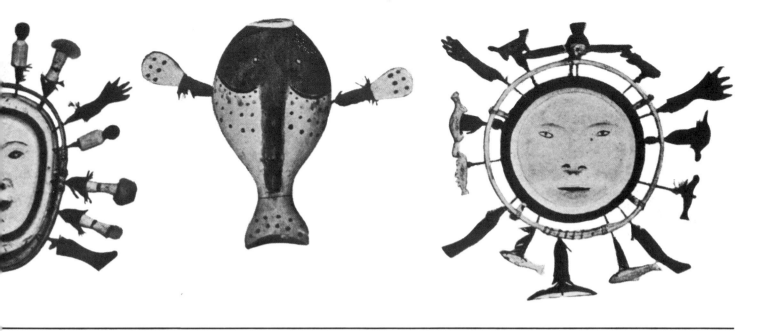

when he is about to get close to her, she disappears mysteriously.

One group of stars outlines the shape of a great bear which the Eskimos call Nanook. He was chased by a pack of hunting dogs who ran so fast that they left the earth and found their way into the sky. Another group of stars resembles a reindeer prancing.

Tonight, if the sky is clear, try to see the great hunter, the moon, in front of his igloo. Look for a shooting star. Perhaps it is one of his dogs leaving the sky in order to visit you.

Above: The images of magical spirits that gave the shaman his powers were depicted on this breastplate.

Right: On long, pitch-black, bitterly cold nights, Eskimos watched the sky and invented stories about the strange dancing lights, which we call the aurora borealis. They carved small ivory figures known as "stargazers" to bring them luck in the darkness.

Above: Sun symbol with wings from the tomb of Ramses III.

Left: This wooden pillar dedicated to the sun god Ra shows him enthroned like a pharaoh and wearing the sun disk on his head. At the top are his two eyes, symbols of eternity. In the middle are many picture symbols known as hieroglyphics.

EGYPT

the force of the sun god ra

In the ancient capital of Heliopolis, in the fertile region of the Nile Delta, there were many gods. One of the most important was Ra, the sun at high noon. Before Ra was born, the world was very dark and cold, but his birth brought light to the world.

Ra first appeared on earth as a scarab beetle which emerged from a beautiful lotus flower. Later, the beetle changed itself into a little boy and when this boy wept, his tears became mankind.

Ra started each morning as a beautiful child. He stepped into his solar boat and started his journey across the sky, which resembled a great starry ocean. When he reached the middle of the sky, he was at the height of his strength—a full grown man. But by late afternoon, he was exhausted.

29

Ra, the sun god of ancient Egypt, had a great watchful eye that never slept and could see the whole world at once. In this 21st Dynasty papyrus, the sun disk encircles the eye of Ra, which is being adored by Thoth and a goddess of the dead.

Ra sailed in a solar boat that was formed of lotus blossoms. Every night, his enemy Apep, a serpent from the underworld, tried to stop the boat, but Thoth, the dogfaced baboon, drove him away. Apep and Thoth are seen at the left and right of this Egyptian painting.

And it was as a weak old man that he left his solar ship and climbed into the night boat for his dangerous journey through the twelve provinces of the underworld. While he was out of the sky, the world was in darkness. The underworld, a dark reflection of the heavens, was the place of the dead. Monstrous creatures and unfriendly spirits lived there.

In the underworld, Ra was always forced to battle his worst enemy, Apep, a huge serpent that lived in the wild

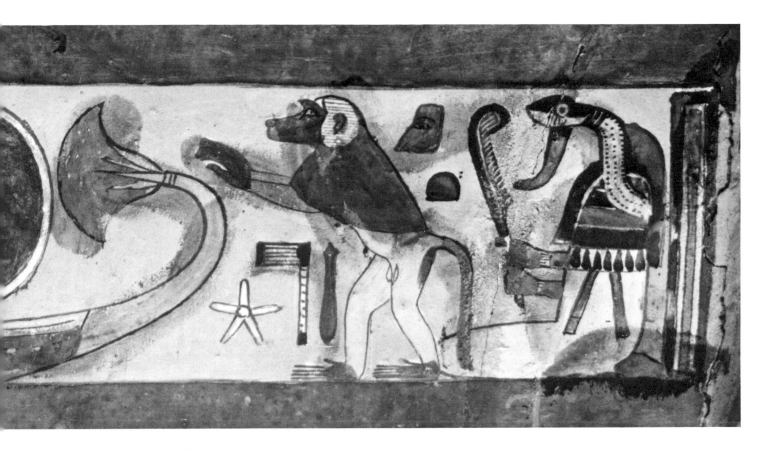

dark waters and tried to stop the passage of the boat. Stormy weather on earth was therefore thought to be a momentary victory of Apep. A total eclipse meant that Apep was swallowing the boat.

Some believed that Apep had been abandoned at the time of Ra's birth. Naturally, he resented being abandoned and forced to live in the cold underworld. For that reason he always revengefully tried to stop the boat from passing through the night and reaching a new day. But Ra, although

Accepted as the descendants of the gods, the pharaohs ruled on earth as the gods ruled the heavens and underworld. Since they believed that the sun god was reborn daily, they also believed in their own rebirth. By their orders, soaring tombs, known as pyramids, were built at Giza. This 4th Dynasty pyramid of Chephren, made of limestone blocks, is 450 feet high.

This 18th Dynasty gold ornament shows the scarab, wearing the sun disk, in his solar boat. He is flanked by Thoth, to whom Ra gave charge of the night sky. Crowned with the full and crescent moons, Thoth is responsible for guiding the boat through the dark, dangerous underworld.

tired from the perpetual battle in the underworld, had the wonderful ability to be reborn each day as a young, strong child.

Ra had a strange and unusual eye. . . . It never slept. It could even separate itself from him and move around.

One day Ra's two children became lost in the terrible waters that surrounded the earth at the beginning of time. The great sun god was very unhappy about the disappearance of his children, and he sent his eye to find them and bring them back to safety.

While the eye was out searching through the waters, Ra replaced him with another bright eye. When the first eye returned with the children, he was furious to see that he had been replaced. But Ra was so overjoyed and grateful to him for bringing back the lost children that he gave him the greatest honor he could think of—he placed him, in the form of a serpent, on his forehead, where the eye could view the entire world.

Perhaps the eye of Ra still watches and protects us today.

Right: The ancient Egyptians believed that Ra was first born in the form of a scarab, a sacred beetle that was the symbol of birth and rebirth. This scarab, carved in gray granite, dates from the time of the Ptolemies.

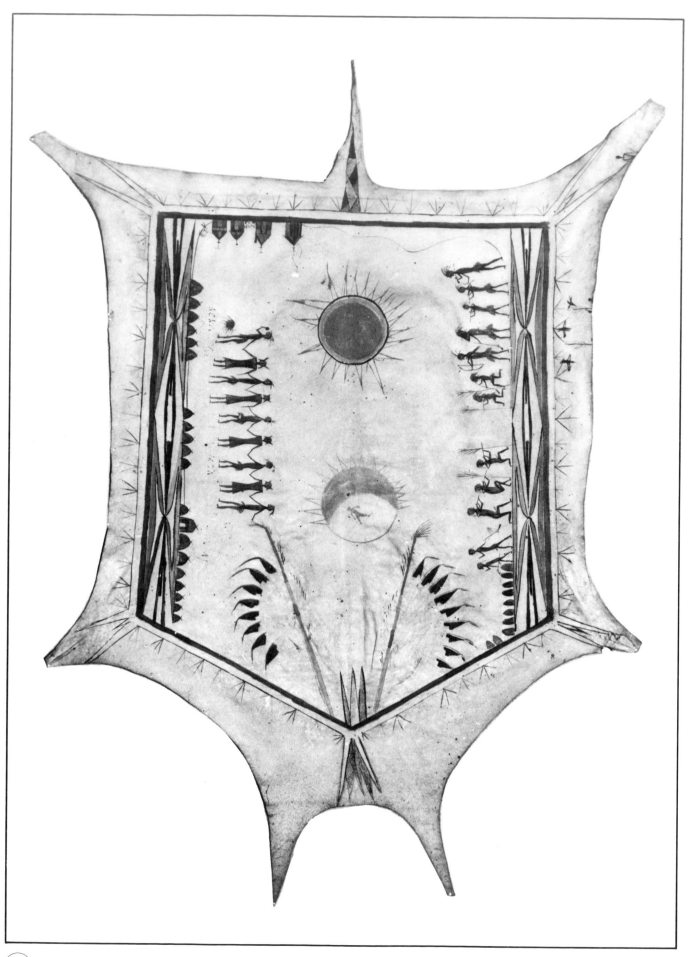

NORTH
AMERICAN
INDIANS
raven and the wonderful
ball of light

Left: Observing the cycles of the sun and moon, the North American Indians could predict the seasons and measure time. The sun and the moon often appear in their art. This battle scene on an 18th-century buffalo skin depicts the sky symbols and shows the man on the moon's surface in the center.

In a very humble house lived a fisherman and his daughter. They had in their house a box that contained a wonderful ball of light.

A powerful creature known as Raven heard about the box and wanted desperately to have the special ball. Raven could assume many different forms whenever he wanted to disguise his real identity. So one day he decided to change himself into a green leaf that was growing on a bush next to the fisherman's house. When the daughter came near the bush, the leaf fell from it and entered her body. Before long, a child was born.

39

The American Indians of the
Northwest Coast believed
that Raven the magician
could disguise himself in
many ways. In one myth
he appears first in the form of
a green leaf and later
changes himself into a little
boy who steals the moon
and throws it into the sky.
This painted wooden mask
from the Kwakiutl tribe
of British Columbia
represents Raven.

All North American Indians, whether farmers, fishermen, or hunters, rely greatly on the sun and the moon. This painted wooden mask from the Bella Coolas of British Columbia represents the sun and the moon together.

As soon as the child could crawl, he began to cry and call for the moon. At first, no one could understand what he wanted. Later, the old fisherman decided to give the child the ball of light to see if that would stop him from crying. He and his daughter carefully opened the ten boxes, each inside another, that preserved the innermost box. By the time they reached the last box, the child had nearly stopped crying and was waiting anxiously to see what was inside. When they finally opened it, the house was suddenly filled with light. Gleefully, the child began to play with the shining white ball.

After a few days, the child began to cry again. He said

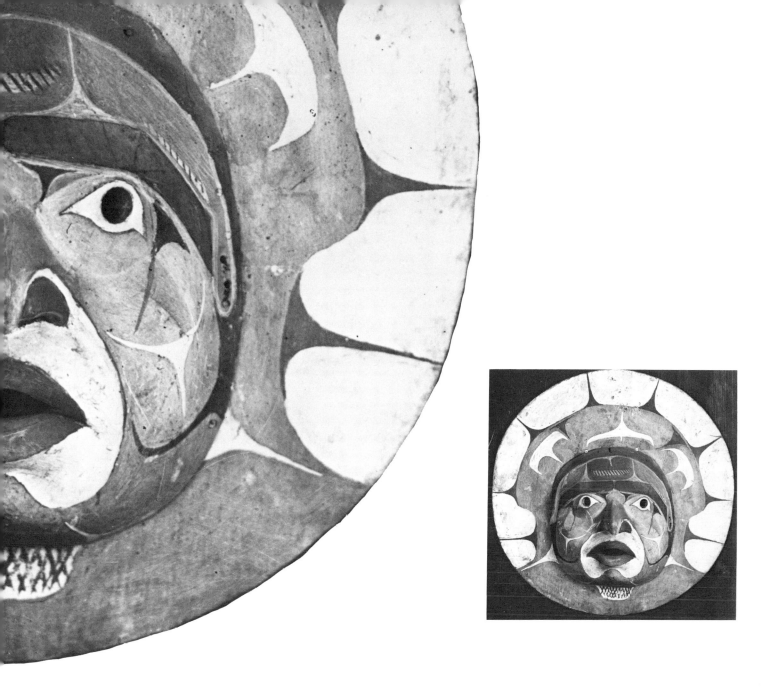

that he couldn't see the night stars in the dark sky because there was no opening in the roof. The kind fisherman again wanted the child to be happy and so he made an opening in the roof. But just when the opening was made, the child changed himself back into Raven and flew away through the opening with the moon in his beak. He traveled for many nights without stopping until he reached a very high mountain top, and then he threw the moon with all his strength into the sky.

So, thanks to Raven's cleverness and determination, the evening sky is no longer dark and lonely and we are blessed with the silver glow of the moon.

Raven's image is everywhere
in Northwest Coast Indian
art. Representations of
Raven, in full face, in profile,
and in various attitudes,
decorate this Kwakiutl
cedar bark mat.

NORTH
AMERICAN
INDIANS
great turtle

In the past, the world was dark because no one had been able to climb the dangerous path to the heavens to put light into the sky.

Great Turtle, the master of all the animals, very much wanted to have some light. One day, Little Turtle, his devoted assistant, decided to try to climb the treacherous path. First she climbed into a black, smoky storm cloud that carried her to the center of the sky. As she went, she collected lightning and gathered it into a great luminous ball. When she had finally gone as high as she could go, she threw the beautiful ball with all her might into the sky.

As she rested from her difficult journey, Little Turtle

This buffalo shield with a design representing a turtle and decorated with feathers was made by Crow Indians of Montana.

looked at the sky and saw how lonely the glowing silver ball was and she noticed that the sky was still too dark. She knew that her job was not finished, so she decided to collect another ball of lightning. She did this and threw it into the sky to join the first ball. The first became the moon and the second, the sun.

Great Turtle was very pleased that Little Turtle had been so successful. Then he had another idea. He wanted the sun and the moon to circle through the sky so that all the world should have light. He called upon his friends, the burrowing animals, to make holes in the corner of the sky, one in the east and one in the west, through which the two lights could pass.

The sun and the moon lived like husband and wife and

one day they quarreled. The sun was angry at the moon for trying to pass through the hole in the sky before him. He was so furious that he forced the moon to disappear for a time into the dark world below. During that time the world was very hot and no one could rest or dream. The moon lost much of her light because of her great sorrow. She became so thin that she was only a sliver of her former self. Little Turtle felt great sympathy for her and mended the sad moon so that she could resume her circling the sky. But the sun was very stubborn and refused to look at her as they passed each other, so she pined away again.

And this has continued throughout time. The moon is full with hope and then slowly pines away in sorrow as the sun passes her by.

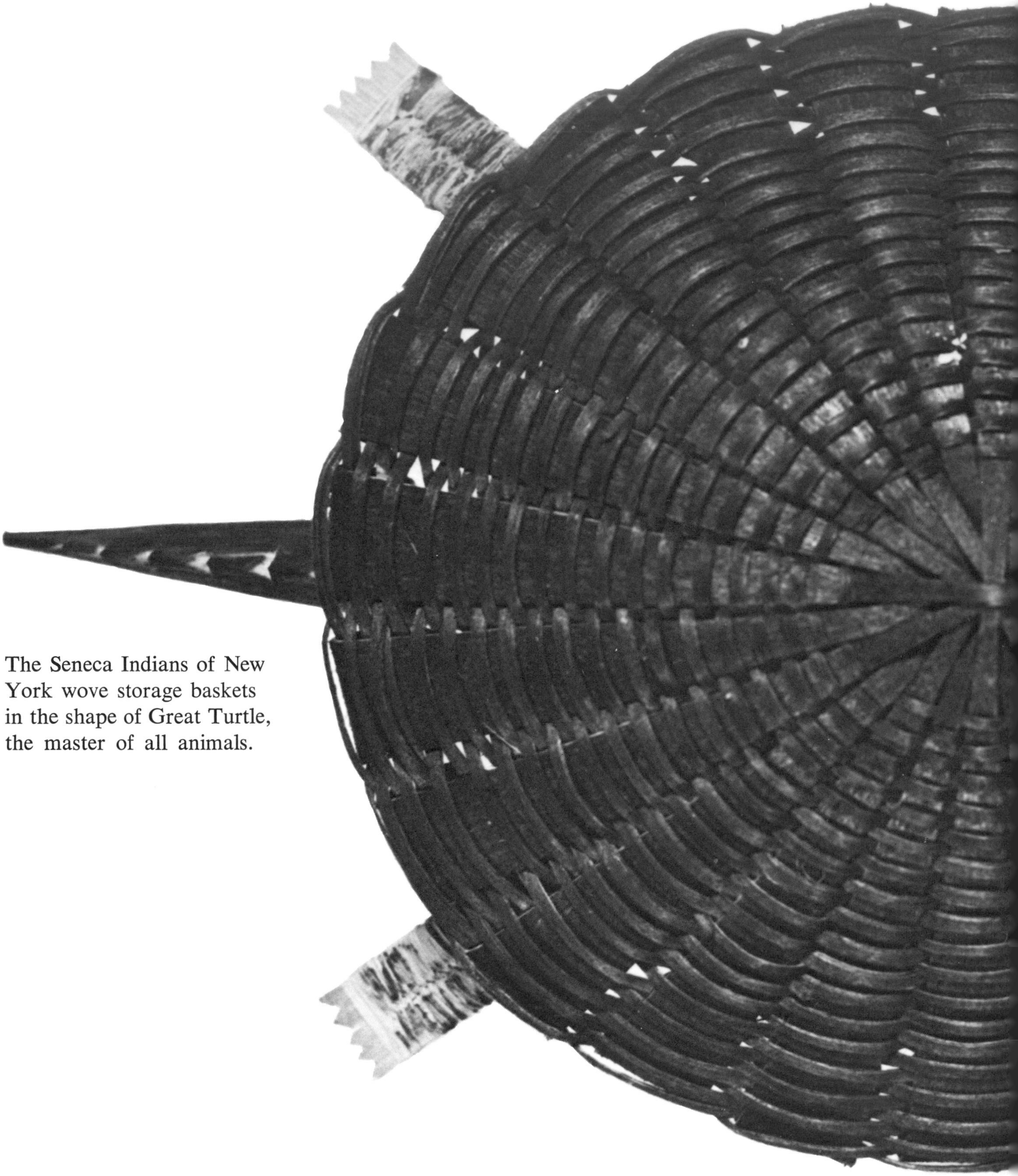

The Seneca Indians of New
York wove storage baskets
in the shape of Great Turtle,
the master of all animals.

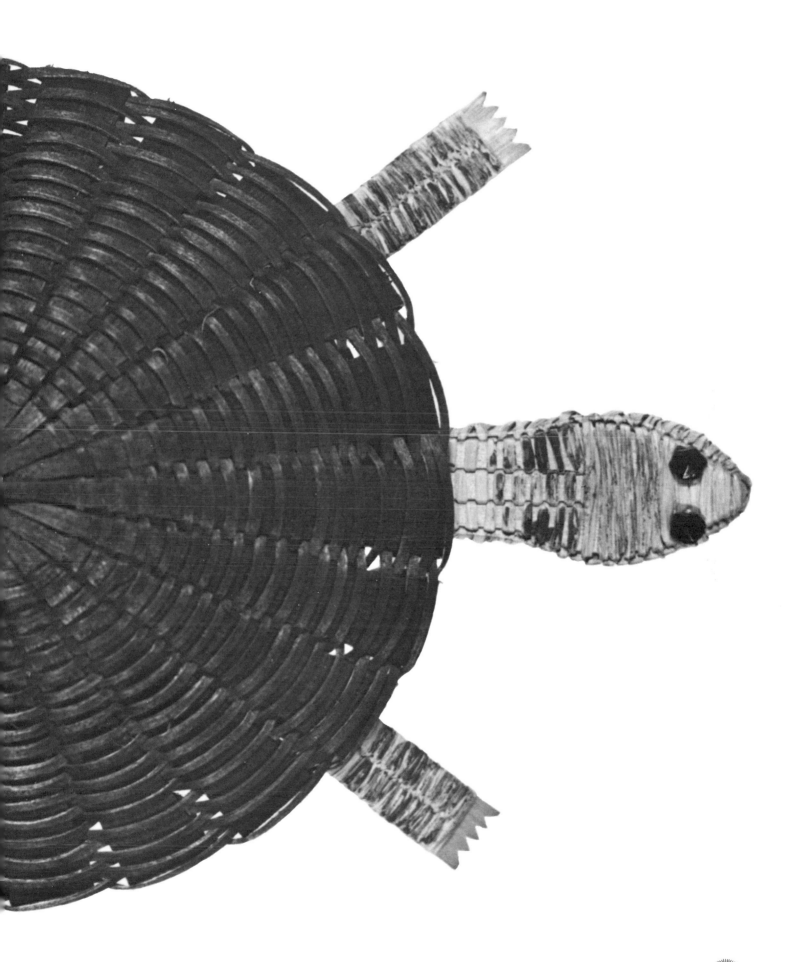

AZTECS

warriors of the sun

One day a lovely goddess was doing her daily chores and thinking of her loneliness and deep sadness. She had many children—the moon and all the hundreds of stars—but they had left her long ago to live in the sky. She missed them terribly and waited every night for them to appear in the dark sky. Although she could see them only from afar, she knew that they were all there and she admired their beauty.

One night, at twilight, when there was an eerie suspense in the air, she was busy sweeping the heavens with her broom in order to make the sky clear for her children to

Left: Quetzalcoatl, the plumed serpent depicted in this stone sculpture, was the Aztec god of the sky, light, and learning.

53

Twelve feet in diameter, this
15th-century Aztec stone
calendar was painted red,
blue, yellow, green, and
other bright colors. The
Aztecs were devoted to the
sun and placed the sun
god in the center of this
calendar.

appear when, suddenly, a beautiful ball of feathers danced in the air before her eyes. . . . She could hardly believe the fabulous blinding colors: turquoise, pink, flaming orange, emerald, and gold. Overjoyed, she tucked the precious ball away in a secret place.

After she had finished all her work, she looked for the magic ball, but it wasn't there and she couldn't understand what had happened. She was almost ready to believe that the feather ball never really existed—that it was just something that her loneliness had led her to imagine. But suddenly she felt the ball move within her and she knew that she was expecting a new baby.

That evening, when her children appeared in the sky, she announced her joyous news. But to her dismay, they were not at all pleased. Instead, they were furious with jealousy and threatened to kill her. They claimed that their presence in the evening sky and the cool, jewel-like silver light that they cast on earth should be satisfaction enough for her.

The poor goddess was filled with despair and began to fear that she would die. She yearned to have another child, but she understood that if she gave birth to this child, the struggle on earth and in the heavens would continue forever. Just as she was wondering what to do, she heard a murmur within her—the voice of someone who was very close and yet very far away. The voice said, "Do not worry, for I will defend you against all."

And it came true. Just as the stars and the moon were about to kill the goddess, a great golden child was born. With the help of his protector, the serpent of fire, the strong child cut off the head of the moon and set the stars into flight.

But after a while, the wise child realized that although he was the powerful sun, man also needed the moon and the stars in the sky in order to cool the earth and give him time to rest. So he brought the stars and moon back to the sky. But they have never forgiven the sun for outshining them, and they always refuse to leave the sky. The sun, must, therefore, battle them daily at dawn. This divine battle continues as it was at the beginning: every day the sun brings a new day of life to mankind by frightening away the moon and the stars with his tremendous light.

Right: The sun is represented on the top of this 15th-century carved stone, and scenes of human sacrifice are carved on the sides. The Aztecs believed that human sacrifice was necessary for nourishing the sun.

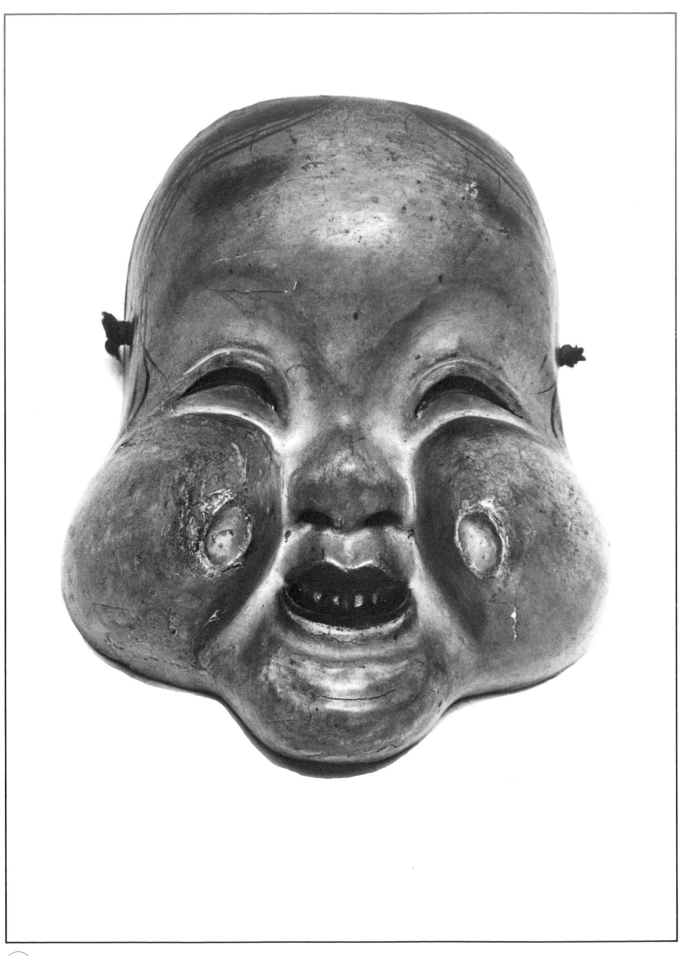

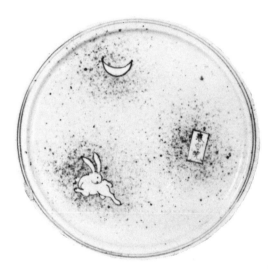

JAPAN

amaterasu, the sun goddess

Before there was light or land, everything was a great swirling ocean mass. A strange substance slowly appeared on this ancient ocean, and from it there came a pair of perfect gods who descended to earth on a beautiful rainbow bridge. They became the parents of the world, and their first children were the islands, waterfalls, mountains, and wind.

One day the great father went to bathe himself in a clear stream. While he was humming and enjoying the cool water, he washed his left eye. By this act, the sun goddess

Left: This Japanese mask depicts the cheerful face of Uzume, goddess of laughter. *Above:* A Japanese plate shows a hare and the moon.

The great glowing sun and
the billowing waves are
painted on this Japanese
six-panel screen.

Amaterasu was formed. Her brilliance and warmth were so great that she was told to rule over the high heavens. When the father bathed his right eye, the moon and the stars were born. Shortly thereafter, the storm god Susano and the thunder god Raiden were created.

The sun and the moon were brother and sister and sat in the celestial land with their backs to one another. The sun shone on half the world and the moon shone on the other half. But the storm god Susano did not get along with his sister the beautiful sun goddess Amaterasu. Because he was born an ugly child, he had always been jealous of her great beauty and good fortune. He had not discovered the beauty within himself and was always attacking his sister in one way or another.

One day Susano visited Amaterasu and said he wanted to apologize for his evil deeds. While apologizing, however, he destroyed her rice fields. Amaterasu was furious and went to hide in a cave, taking her warmth and light with her and leaving the world dark and cold. When she was able to be by herself for a while, her anger left her and she felt more peaceful. In fact, she liked her solitude so much that she refused to come out for what seemed an endless time to the people on earth. Finally, in the hope of enticing her to reappear, a group of gods and goddesses led by Uzume, goddess of laughter, came near her cave and performed a beautiful, strange, festive dance. The sun goddess was so overcome by curiosity that she came out of the cave to watch them. Unexpectedly, she saw her own reflection in a mirror that they had hung on a tree so that she would again witness her own beauty and realize their need for her.

Since then, the whole world has experienced both day and night, and the storm god Susano has been careful not to offend his sister, the great sun goddess.

Left: To the people of Dahomey, the sun and moon were twin brother and sister, living happily in the heavens as the father and mother of all the stars and planets.

Above: Ashanti women carried moon-faced fertility figures to bring them luck in childbirth.

AFRICA
the twins

The people of Dahomey have two favorite gods, Mawu and her twin brother Lisa. Mawu, the moon, is a beautiful woman who lives in the west. She is gentle to man and controls the night. Lisa, the sun, lives in the east. He is very fierce and brutal. Together, they are the perfect balance of elements. They respect each other very much and enjoy protecting mankind.

For a long time they were very sad because they had no children. But one day they came together during an eclipse and soon became the parents of seven sets of twins—all gods and goddesses—the planets.

That is the reason that whenever there is an eclipse of the sun and the moon, the people of Dahomey say Mawu and Lisa are making love.

AFRICA
the bat

In the beginning, the world was never really dark or cold. The sun shone during the day and the moon gave twilight to the night. One day, God asked the bat to carry a covered basket filled with darkness to the moon. He said that the bat should not ask why but should just do as he was told. Later, God himself would go to the moon to explain what to do with the basket.

On his way, however, the bat became hungry and tired, and he stopped. He put the basket down and ventured off to look for food. While he was gone, some animals found the basket sitting by the side of the road. They were overcome with curiosity and opened the basket, letting darkness escape throughout the world.

As soon as he saw the darkness, the bat realized at once that he was responsible. In an effort to be forgiven for his grave mistake, he now sleeps during the day and flies madly around at night, trying to catch darkness and deliver it to the moon. But he has never succeeded, and because he did not realize the importance of his God-given task, darkness still covers the whole world.

Left: A Yoruba mother of twins used this male twin figure, clothed in cowrie shells, cloth, and beads, to protect her children's health.

This Ekoi ceremonial
headdress of a ram is made
of wood, skin, twine,
cloth, nails, paint,
and basketry.

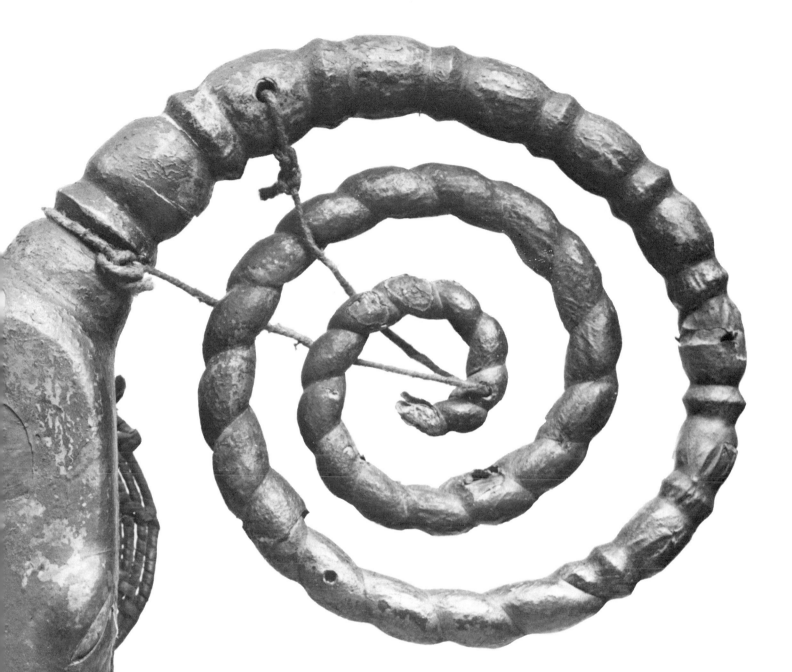

AFRICA
the ram

The Dagomba people believe that the sun is surrounded by a wonderful, bustling marketplace—the halo that we sometimes see. This is the home of a very temperamental ram. When he is angry, he stamps his feet and causes thunder. When he shakes his tail, lightning flashes. Rain is the hair falling from the ram's tail. The wind is the ram playfully rushing around the marketplace.

INCAS

children of the sun

Left: People of Peru used this beaten gold calendar between 800 B.C. and A.D. 200. Around the edges are gods associated with the sun.

Above: This engraved gold plaque is probably from an Inca temple.

Thousands of years ago, in the majestic hills that surround Lake Titicaca in Peru, men lived in caves and hollows like wild beasts, eating roots, wild plants, and animals. Even the peaceful llamas and alpacas were afraid of these early people because they were so uncivilized.

The great sun saw men living in this primitive state without homes or religion and totally unable to cultivate the land. He felt sorry for them and sent his two children, Mama Occlo and Manco Capac, to an island in Lake Titicaca to show men the arts of civilized life and to teach the religion of the sun.

The sun gave the two beautiful children a long golden rod to take with them. They were instructed to sink the rod into the soil, and the place where the rod sank completely was to be the sacred city of the sun.

The two children journeyed far into the country, trying over and over again to sink the golden rod into the soil. It would not bury itself until they reached the valley of Cuzco. The children then knew that this was to be the sacred city of the sun.

They then set out to bring people to this place. The brother went to the north and the sister to the south. When all the people they could find were gathered together, the children began to teach them to live in towns and villages. Manco Capac taught the men to cultivate the soil, to make ploughs, and to irrigate the earth. Mama Occlo taught the women to sew, weave, and cook. The beautiful llamas and alpacas were no longer afraid.

The people worshipped Mama Occlo and Manco Capac because they were the children of the sun. The two children are the ancestors of the Inca people whose kings were believed to be the sun's relatives, and therefore also divine.

Perhaps the rod is still in the valley of Cuzco today, buried deep down somewhere near the center of the earth.

Right: Machu Picchu, the "lost city" of the Incas, has more than a hundred stairways, the most prominent of which leads from the central plaza to the towering peak of Huayna Picchu. At the top is a platform known as "the hitching post of the sun."

宋張擇端白雲出岫圖 嶺南潘氏珍藏

74

CHINA

ten suns, twelve moons

Left: This 12th-century Sung Dynasty silk scroll depicts a landscape similar to the sacred Valley of Light.

Above: On this 9th-century bronze mirror the toad and the hare, sitting on the moon under a cassia tree, watch the evening stars.

At the farthest eastern edge of the world, in a valley called the Valley of Light is a clear blue lake with water as fresh and peaceful as the first seconds of dawn. Although our feet cannot take us there, if we close our eyes our mind can travel to this sacred place of the ten suns. We can see the beautiful po tree with its transparent purple berries against a pale pink sky. The air is cool and misty, for here it is always dawn.

Every morning ten golden youths are bathed by their mother in the sparkling lake water. Refreshed from their bath, they joyfully climb the great po tree and announce the beginning of a new day. Only one sun reaches the very top of the tree, where he finds his mother waiting. Bursting with energy, he climbs into a chariot and is drawn across the sky of day by golden dragons with red teeth and emerald green eyes. His mother drives the chariot while the strong sun looks out on the world with sharp guardian eyes. Sometimes the sun becomes very intense, particularly when he reaches the center of the sky.

After some time, the chariot reaches its destination, Mount Yen-Tzu, in the west. The dragons are unyoked and the tired sun descends to earth by climbing down a magnificent jo tree. He yields to this moment of peace and allows the world to become dark. Then he greets the cooling delicate light of the moon and stars. While the flowers of the beautiful jo tree begin to glow and light the sky and the moon appears in the west, the sun makes his way mysteriously back to rejoin his brothers, the other suns, at the eastern edge of the world.

Twelve silver maidens are moons both delicate and powerful. Drawn also by a chariot, one moon crosses the

Right: Hares, popular in Chinese art, are seen here in a Sung Dynasty painting of about A.D. 1200. The three hares are huddled together and one lifts a paw and looks toward the moon.

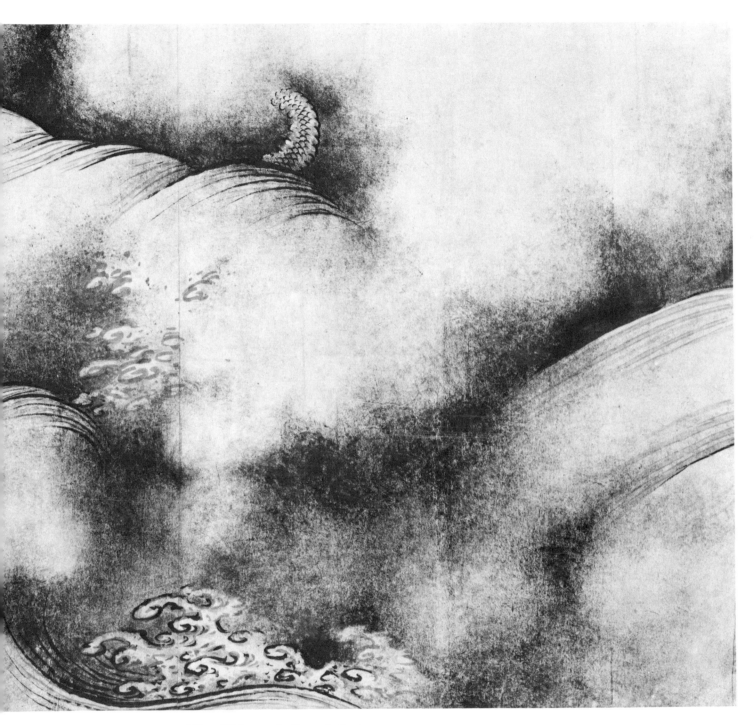

The Chinese believed that
golden dragons pulled the sun
chariot across the sky.
Those depicted on this
13th-century Nine-Dragon
Scroll are like great
waves and clouds.

sky, casting a soft silver light on the earth that is cooling below. When the moonlight is full, it is so intense that foxes, poets, and lovers stay awake all night and watch sharp shadows dance about.

The moon, made of water, is the home of a hare and his friend the toad. They sit together beneath the cassia tree because they enjoy its cinnamon scent and can watch the stars best from this spot.

Every night, the hare and toad watch two particular stars, who are husband and wife, wave to each other. These two stars are the eternal young man, the celestial cowherd, and his beautiful unchanging wife, the heavenly weaver girl. They now lie on opposite sides of the celestial river, the Milky Way, but they have not always been separated.

Once their marriage was an ideal courtship which seemed to have no end. They passed the time gazing contentedly into each other's eyes. The weaver girl's loom collected dust; the cowherd's flocks were unwatched.

But the other gods punished them for their neglectful behavior and separated them. Only on one day each year—the seventh day of the seventh month—is the heavenly weaver girl allowed to cross the celestial river to visit her amorous husband. Her bridge is a curious one: it is composed of magpies who gather together to support her fragile weight. Should it rain on that day, however, the birds will leave to seek shelter, and the saddened lady must wait another year before she can see her husband.

Every day, each goes to the edge of the celestial river hoping to see the other. But they never even get a glimpse, for the distance is too great and the glaring reflections of the other stars in the river are too strong.

Right: A Chinese painting of magpies on a wintry bough. The heavenly weaver girl crossed a bridge formed of magpies to visit her husband the celestial cowherd.

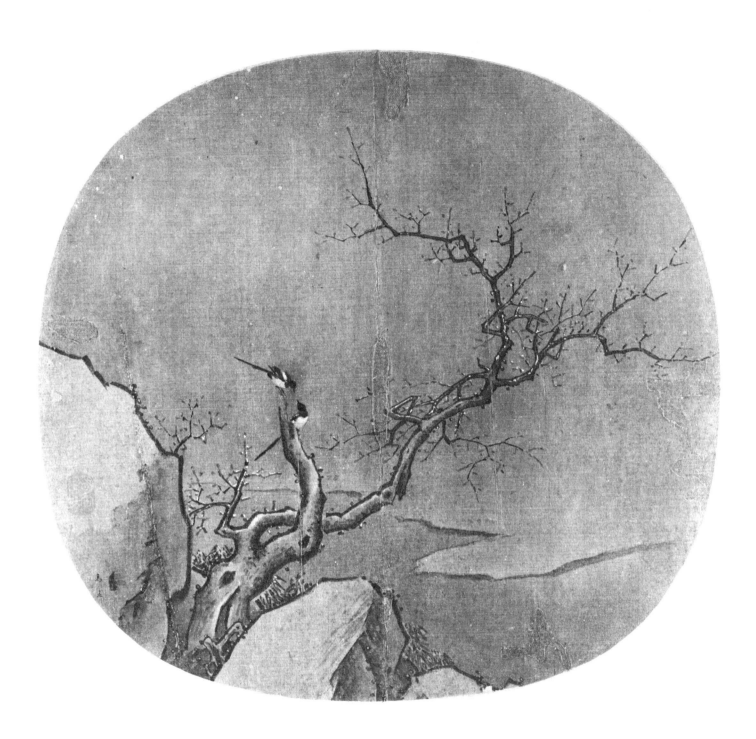

This Sung Dynasty jade
screen shows the heavenly
weaver girl (*left*), with
her loom, and the celestial
cowherd (*right*), with
his ox and plough, who
were so much in love that
they neglected their
duties. The other gods,
angry at their irresponsibility,
punished them by separating
them forever.

The birth of the sun and moon has different meanings in various cultures. Yet there is one common message behind all these stories.

The world was not meant to be enclosed in darkness. For that reason, the sun and the moon were created to bring light to the world.

Light is more than the absence of darkness. It is knowledge, beauty, joy, and freedom.

People also were not meant to live in darkness. Within each of us there is a light, and it is our responsibility to let this light shine.

Photographs

Page 38: 18th-century North American Indian buffalo skin. Musée de l'Homme, Paris.

Pages 40, 41: Kwakiutl painted wooden mask of Raven. British Columbia. Museum of the American Indian, Heye Foundation, New York.

Pages 42, 43: Bella Coola mask of sun and moon. British Columbia. American Museum of Natural History, New York.

Page 44: Kwakiutl cedar bark mat with painted decoration representing Raven. British Columbia. Museum of the American Indian, Heye Foundation, New York.

Pages 46, 47, 49: Crow Indian buffalo hide shield with a turtle design. Montana. Museum of the American Indian, Heye Foundation, New York.

Pages 50, 51: Seneca basketry turtle. New York State. Museum of the American Indian, Heye Foundation, New York.

Page 52: Aztec stone sculpture of Quetzalcoatl. 13th-15th century. Photographie Giraudon, Paris.

Pages 54, 55: Aztec stone calendar. 1427-92. Roger-Viollet, Paris.

Page 57: 15th-century Aztec carved stone. Roger-Viollet, Paris.

Page 58: Japanese Noh theater mask of Uzume. Wood and painted lacquer. Collection Katherine Komaroff. Photograph by Akira Kokubo.

Page 59: 17th-century Japanese plate. British Museum, London.

Pages 60, 61: Japanese six-panel painted screen of sun and billowing waves. Metropolitan Museum of Art, New York, Gift of Mrs. Edward G. Robinson, 1950.

Page 62: The Wave. Woodcut by Hokusai (1760-1849). Photographie Giraudon, Paris.

Page 64: Dahomeyan painted wooden statue of twins. Musée de l'Homme, Paris.

Page 65: Ashanti wooden fertility figure. Ghana. Museum of Primitive Art, New York. Photograph by Lisa Little.

Page 66: Yoruba male twin figure. Wood, cowries, cloth, beads. Nigeria. Museum of Primitive Art, New York. Photograph by Charles Uht.

Pages 68, 69: Ekoi ram's-head headdress. Wood, skin, twine, cloth, nails, paint, basketry. Nigeria. Museum of Primitive Art, New York. Photograph by Charles Uht.

Page 70: Gold disk calendar. Peru. 800 B.C.-A.D. 200. Museum of the American Indian, Heye Foundation, New York.

Page 71: Engraved gold plaque (fragment). Peru. Roger-Viollet, Paris.

Page 73: Machu Picchu, Peru, the lost city of the Incas. Roger-Viollet, Paris.

Page 74: Chinese Sung Dynasty painting, hanging scroll painted on silk. 12th century. Metropolitan Museum of Art, New York, Fletcher Fund, 1947.

Page 75: 9th-century Chinese bronze mirror. Victoria and Albert Museum, London.

Page 77: Sung Dynasty painting of hares. About A.D. 1200. Metropolitan Museum of Art, New York.

Pages 78, 79: The Great Nine-Dragon Scroll (detail). 13th century. Boston Museum of Fine Arts, Boston.

Page 81: Chinese painting of wintry bough with magpies. Metropolitan Museum of Art, New York, Fletcher Fund, 1947.

Pages 82, 83: Jade screen (two sides). Ch'ing Dynasty, 1662-1722. Seattle Art Museum, Eugene Memorial Collection. Photograph by Earl Fields.

DATE DUE
